The Cornell University.

FIRST GENERAL ANNOUNCEMENT.

THE CORNELL UNIVERSITY.

AT ITHACA, N. Y.

FIRST GENERAL ANNOUNCEMENT.

TRUSTEES.

*HIS EXCELLENCY, REUBEN E. FENTON, *Governor.*
*HIS HONOR STEWART L. WOODFORD, *Lieutenant-Governor.*
*HON. EDMUND L. PITTS, *Speaker.*
*GEN. MARSENA R. PATRICK, *President State Agricultural Society.*
*HON. VICTOR M. RICE, *Superintendent of Public Instruction.*
*HON. EZRA CORNELL, *Chairman of Board of Trustees.*
*HON. ANDREW D. WHITE, *President of the University.*
*FRANCIS M. FINCH, ESQ., *Librarian Cornell Public Library.*
*ALONZO B. CORNELL, ESQ., ITHACA.

HON. HORACE GREELEY, NEW YORK.
HON. EDWIN D. MORGAN, NEW YORK.
HON. ERASTUS BROOKS, NEW YORK.
HON. WILLIAM KELLY, RHINEBECK.
GEN. J. MEREDITH READ, ALBANY.
HON. GEORGE H. ANDREWS, SPRINGFIELD, OTSEGO CO.
HON. ABRAM B. WEAVER, DEERFIELD, ONEIDA CO.
HON. CHARLES J. FOLGER, GENEVA.
HON. EDWIN B. MORGAN, AURORA.
HON. JOHN M. PARKER, OWEGO.
HIRAM SIBLEY, ESQ., ROCHESTER.
HON. JOSIAH B. WILLIAMS, ITHACA.
HON. GEORGE W. SCHUYLER, ITHACA, *Treas. of the University.*
WILLIAM ANDRUS, ESQ., ITHACA.
JOHN MCGRAW, ESQ., ITHACA.

*TRUSTEES EX-OFFICIO.

CORNELL UNIVERSITY.

FIRST GENERAL ANNOUNCEMENT.

THE first term of the CORNELL UNIVERSITY, at Ithaca, N. Y., will open on the last Wednesday in September, 1868, with the inauguration of the President and Professors.

The examination of candidates for admission will be conducted by the Professors elect in the several departments, on the Monday and Tuesday preceding.

Though students can be received at a later period, it is greatly desired that they appear on Monday and Tuesday as above.

The organization of Departments, Courses and Classes will immediately follow the inauguration exercises, and there will be no delay in the commencement of instruction.

Departments and Courses will be organized as follows:

DIVISION OF SPECIAL SCIENCES AND ARTS.

1. The Department of Agriculture.
2. " " The Mechanic Arts.
3. " " Civil Engineering.
4. " " Military Engineering and Tactics.
5. " " Mining and Practical Geology.
6. " " History, Social and Political Science.

In all the instruction in these Departments a constant effort will be made to educate men to speedily become *practically useful in developing the resources and in aiding in the general progress of the country.*

In the DEPARTMENT OF AGRICULTURE, science and practice will go together, not to rear a body of *amateur* agriculturists, but to bring scientific methods to bear in ordinary agriculture, so that *tried by an economic test* the result shall be to advance the prosperity of the country. Special attention will be given to the education of young men, ambitious to become instructors and professors in the numerous agricultural colleges now rising in nearly all the states of the Union.

In the DEPARTMENT OF THE "MECHANIC ARTS," science will also be applied to practice; fitting men to take positions of influence and usefulness, in developing the manufacturing and mechanical resources and interests of the country. Special attention will be paid to the practical education of those who wish to take charge of manufactories and work-shops of various sorts.

In the DEPARTMENT OF CIVIL ENGINEERING the same idea of making thoroughly scientific men for speedy practical use will be carried out.

The DEPARTMENT OF MILITARY ENGINEERING AND TACTICS it is hoped to place under the supervision of graduates of the National Academy at West Point.

The DEPARTMENT OF MINING AND PRACTICAL GEOLOGY has for its aim the fitting of men to develop the vast mineral resources of the nation. When it is considered what immense losses have been incurred under the management of unscientific or half-scientific men, the importance of this Department will be recognized. Situated as the University is near one of the greatest mining districts of the United States, it presents special attractions to all students desiring real preparation for work of the kind contemplated.

In the DEPARTMENT OF HISTORY, SOCIAL AND POLITICAL SCIENCE, the need of the country for a higher and more thorough education for the public service, will be constantly kept in view. Principles as thought out by Economists, Statesmen and Historians will be constantly applied to what has been actually wrought out in society. The trustees will endeavor, in questions of Political Economy, upon which good and able men differ, to have both sides ably presented and discussed. No attempt will be made, however, to proselyte students to any peculiar or partisan views.

DIVISION OF SCIENCE, LITERATURE AND THE ARTS IN GENERAL.

1. First General Course, or "Modern Course."

This will extend through four years. To Modern Languages, which have become so indispensable in a good education, will be mainly assigned the place and labor usually given to Ancient Languages. The course will be suited to the needs of students, so far as possible, by the allowance of options between studies in the latter years of the course, on a plan somewhat similar to that lately adopted at Harvard University.

2. "Modern Course Abridged."

This course will extend through three years. This, as well as the abridged courses which follow, are intended to meet the needs of those students who have not time for a full general course. It will give the *main* studies of the extended course, the *subordinate* studies being omitted so as to decrease the time one year.

3. Second General Course, or "Combined Course."

This course will extend through four years. In this the languages studied will be Latin and German, the remainder of the course being essentially the same as the "General Course." To those who wish to make a thorough study of Modern Languages this course will be valuable, as combining the most useful parts, practically, of the courses usually pursued in Colleges, with a broader course; giving the two sides of all the great Modern Languages and literatures, including our own, and aiding the scientific student greatly in the literature and nomenclature of science.

4. "Combined Course Abridged."

This will extend through three years. Its name explains its character.

5. Third General Course, or "Classical Course."

This will be mainly like the "First General Course," with the option of Ancient Languages for Modern.

6. "Scientific Course."

This will extend through three years, affording a general scientific preparation for either of the first four departments in the "First Division," as named above. A special effort will be made to bring this department fully up to the needs of the times, both by the course adopted and by the professors elected to maintain it.

7. Scientific Course Abridged.

This will extend through two years. Its name explains its character.

8. Optional Course.

This is similar to that allowed American students in the greater German Universities; also like the "Select Course" at the University of Michigan; and which, in both cases, has been very successful. In this course the student, on consultation with friends and the appropriate instructors, selects any three studies for which he may be fitted, from the whole range of studies pursued in the entire University, follows them up to such point as may be agreed upon, and receives, from the Governing Board of the University, at the completion of his work, a certificate, showing the extent of the course he has taken.

9. Degrees, Diplomas and Certificates.

Appropriate degrees, attested by diplomas or certificates, will be conferred upon all students passing satisfactorily through any of the above named departments or courses. But it is thoroughly to be understood that no distinction will be made between the courses extending through four years, as to the name, character or value of the degree or diploma, and the trustees pledge themselves to use every effort to prevent any caste-spirit in any department or course as compared with another.

REQUIREMENTS FOR ADMISSION.

General Requirements.

All candidates for admission to any department or course must present satisfactory evidences of good moral character.

All candidates for admission to any of the special departments in the "*First Division*" must be at least sixteen years of age. All candidates for admission to any of the courses of the "*Second Division*" must be at least fifteen years of age.

Candidates for advanced standing will be examined in the previous studies of the course which they purpose to enter, and if they come from another College or University will present certificates of honorable dismission.

Entering the University will be considered a pledge to obey its rules and regulations.

Candidates for admission to any department or course must have received a good common English education, and be morally, mentally and physically qualified to pursue to advantage the course of study to which they propose to give their attention.*

Special Requirements.

1. In the Department of Civil Engineering and Architecture, Military Engineering and Tactics, and Mining and Practical Geology. In addition to the general requirements candidates will be examined in the whole of Elementary and Plane Geometry.

* The same qualifications as those named for the Lawrence Scientific School at Cambridge.

2. For the "COMBINED COURSE" in the Second Division, in which Latin is taken as an optional study in place of one of the Modern Languages, in addition to the general requirements the candidate will be examined in Cæsar's Commentaries, Cicero's Select Orations, six books of the Æneid and forty-five exercises in Arnold's Prose Composition, or in a course equivalent to this.

3. For the "THIRD GENERAL COURSE," or "CLASSICAL COURSE," an examination will be made similar to that for entering the first year at the existing Colleges of a good grade.

OF CANDIDATES IMPERFECTLY PREPARED.

For candidates found to be of good mental quality, but defective in preparation, provision will be made for special preparatory instruction in a department separate and distinct, but under the control and direction of the University Faculty, until such students are fully competent to enter the University. Students intending to enter are urged to give their main attention, from the time of receiving this circular, to strengthening themselves in a "*sound, ordinary English education;*" such as can be obtained in every good public school or academy. Let their efforts be laid out in perfecting themselves in the following course:

In English Grammar, the general practical principles, with the strictest attention to exercises in Orthography. In English composition each applicant should take pains to cultivate skill and facility. To this end frequent and brief essays and impromptu compositions, oral and written, are recommended. In Geography, the leading facts of General Geography, with special attention to the Geography of Europe and America, to be learned, not by "parroting" from text books, but by common-sense study of any atlas, taking one map after another, fastening into the mind the leading, physical and political features in the Geography of each continent and of each country, and finally grouping them mentally together. To this end map drawing will be found of the greatest use. Three weeks' study, in this way, will do more than three years study after the ordinary method. In Arithmetic, attention should be especially directed to fundamental principles. These should be clearly apprehended, and fairly fixed in the student's mind. In view of the course to be pursued in the University, too much importance cannot be given to a thorough preliminary drill in Mental Arithmetic.

Good health, good habits, and a good thorough education in the common English branches, are then the simple requirements for admission. Every failure in institutions for higher education may be traced to a defect in one of these respects. On these, as a basis, the University pledges itself to build a good superstructure.

Fees for Tuition.

The fees for tuition to persons not exempt under the charter as "State Students," are ten dollars for each term, or thirty dollars for the year. Neither matriculation fees nor initiation fees are required.

In special cases of students of decided merit, who are proven to be in great need, a remission may be made, either wholly or in part of tuition fees, such remission being considered as a *loan*, the student giving a note or promise to pay them so soon as he shall become able after leaving the University. In all other cases payment for each term must be made in advance. Students will be held responsible for any injury which may be done by them to the University property.

Payments for Materials used in Laboratory Practice.

Chemicals and other materials used in laboratory practice will be charged to the student using them at actual cost price.

"State Students."

In the original act of incorporation of the University is the following section:

"§ 9. The several departments of study in the said University shall be open to applicants for admission thereto at the lowest rates of expense consistent with its welfare and efficiency, and without distinction as to rank, class, previous occupation or locality. But with a view to equalize its advantages to all parts of the State, the institution shall annually receive students, one from each Assembly District in the State, to be selected as hereinafter provided, and shall give them instruction in any or in all the prescribed branches of study in any department of said institution, free of any tuition fee, or of any incidental charges, to be paid to said University, unless such incidental charges shall have been made to compensate for damages needlessly or purposely done by the students to the property of said University. The said free instruction shall moreover be accorded to said students in consideration of their superior ability, and as a reward for superior scholarship in the academies and public schools of this State. Said students shall be selected as the Legislature may, from time to time, direct, and until otherwise ordered, as follows: The School Commissioner or Commissioners of each county, and the Board of Education of each city, or those performing the duties of such a board, shall select annually the best scholar from each academy and each public school of their respective counties or cities as candidates for the University scholarship. The candidates thus selected in each county or city shall meet at such time and place in the year as the Board of Supervisors of the county shall appoint, to be examined by a board consisting of the School Commissioner or Commissioners of the county, or by the said Board of Education of the cities, with such other persons as the Supervisors shall appoint, who shall examine said candidates and determine which of them are the best scholars; and the Board of Supervisors shall then select therefrom to the number of one for each assembly district in said county or city, and furnish the candidates thus selected with a certificate of such selection, which certificate shall entitle said student to admission to said University, subject to the examination and approval of the Faculty of said University. In making these selections preference shall be given (where other qualifications are equal) to the sons of those who have died in the military or naval service of the United States; consideration shall be had also of the physical ability of the candidate. Whenever any student selected as above described shall have been, from any cause, removed from the University before the expiration of the time for which he was selected, then one of the competitors to his place in the University from his district may be elected to succeed him therein, as the School Commissioner or Commissioners of the county of his residence, or the Board of Education of the city of his residence, may direct."

Under this the Superintendent of Public Instruction will, at an early day, issue a circular defining the duties of School Commissioners regarding the examinations under this act, and making suggestions as to the best manner of conducting them.

All students presenting themselves at the University with a certificate, such as is contemplated in the section above cited, showing that after an examination he has been adjudged the "best scholar," will be admitted to any department or course for which he is fitted, and continued for four years, or as long as he shall profitably employ his time in the University, free of all matriculation fees, term taxes, or any other payment for tuition.

Rooms.

Suites of rooms will be provided, in the College buildings and near the grounds, sufficient for the accommodation of about two hundred students. Each suite in the buildings consists of a study with bed-rooms and closets adjoining. They are large and convenient, with careful provision for heat and ventilation, and no study or bed-room has been or will be constructed without *direct* communication with the outer light and air.

It is intended, at the expense of the University, to provide neat and durable furniture. The rent of rooms and furniture will range from seventy-five cents to one dollar per week, according to the occupation of the suite of rooms by two students or by three. Rooms can also be obtained, at reasonable rates, with families in the town.

Board.

Board can be obtained in the village at moderate rates. Probably good board could be secured, at a lower price, by the formation of clubs among the students. The University Steward will be authorized, in such case, to aid clubs, by the purchase of stores for them at wholesale, and by securing rooms.

Fuel.

The direct communication with the neighboring coal mines gives advantages in this respect. The University Steward will purchase coal at wholesale and retail it to students at wholesale prices.

OFFICERS AND EQUIPMENT OF THE UNIVERSITY.

Faculty.

A resident Faculty will be in readiness which, it is believed, will command the confidence of all friends of advanced and extended education. In addition to these, it is intended to secure, as non-resident professors, a number of gentlemen especially distinguished to deliver courses of lectures in their several departments. Several gentlemen of acknowledged eminence in science, literature and the practical arts, have already signified their willingness to accept such positions, and it is intended to announce the names of the Faculty, resident and non-resident, through the public prints early in the summer of 1868.

Buildings.

One large stone building, 165 by 50 feet, and four stories in height, has already been erected; another of the same size is in progress. In these, beside dormitories, are library, lecture and recitation rooms, over thirty in number, and of various sizes.

Laboratories.

There will be two laboratories well equipped, one under the direction of the Professor of Agricultural Chemistry, and the other under the Professor of General Chemistry.

Collections.

The University already possesses the Jewett collection in Palæontology and Geology, at a cost of ten thousand dollars, and has received a donation from the State of a collection of duplicates from the State Geological collection, and has funds now in hand to make large additional collections for illustration in the different departments.

Libraries.

The trustees feel warranted in stating that the University will commence with a scientific and general library sufficient for the immediate wants of Faculty and Students, and constant appropriations will be made for its increase.

Student Labor and Practical Instruction in Agriculture.

There is much labor to be done upon the farm attached to the Agricultural department, and a large number of students can be employed from one to three hours a day, at fair prices. Shortly after the organization of the University, the University Steward will organize a voluntary corps for systematized and remunerated labor, under the direction of the Professor of Agriculture and Engineering.

Student Labor and Practical Instruction in the Mechanic Arts.

It is intended to erect workshops upon the University property where students, under proper direction, can have practical instruction in Mechanic Arts. The first of these will be a workshop fitted with the proper machinery for working in wood and iron, in which students can labor at fair prices upon agricultural implements and machinery in general, and upon models for the University collections of machinery and apparatus.

Accomplished artisans will superintend this work, and the attention of those young men who would qualify themselves, by scientific study, for the most responsible and remunerative positions as master mechanics and superintendents of workshops, is invited to this feature in the course of practical instruction.

Prizes.

The following prizes are offered by the Founder of the University to aid meritorious students :

To the student of the Volunteer labor Corps in Agriculture, who, without neglecting his other University duties, shall have shown himself most efficient, practically and scientifically, upon the University farm, ... $50 00
To the second in merit, ... 20 00
To the third in merit,......................... 10 00

To the student of the Volunteer labor Corps in the Mechanic Arts, who, without neglecting his other University duties, shall have shown himself most efficient, practically and scientifically, in the University workshops,...... $50 00
To the second in merit, ... 20 00
To the third in merit,......................... 10 00

The above shall be known as the "Founder's prizes."

The following prizes are offered by the President of the University to aid meritorious students:

To the student showing the most satisfactory progress in the "Modern Course" during the first year,....... $50 00
To the second in merit, ... 20 00

To the student showing the most satisfactory progress in the "Combined Course" during the first year,...... $50 00
To the second in merit, ... 20 00

To the most meritorious student in Chemistry, as applied to Agriculture, ... $50 00
To the second in merit, ... 20 00

To the most meritorious student in Practical Mechanics and Physics, ... $50 00
To the second in merit, ... 20 00

To the most meritorions student in General History,. $50 00
To the second in merit, ... 20 00

To the most meritorious student in Modern History,. $50 00
To the second in merit, ... 20 00

To the writer of the best English Essay,............ $50 00
To the second in merit, ... 20 00

To the student who, without neglecting his other duties as a member of the University, shall make the most satisfactory development in physical culture, ... $50 00
To the second in merit,........................ 20 00
To the third in merit,.......................... 10 00

The committees of examination reserve the right to withhold a prize where the competition shows a standard not sufficiently elevated.

The above shall be known as the "President's prizes."

ORIGIN OF THE UNIVERSITY.

The establishment of the Cornell University is due to the combined bounty of the General Government and of the Hon. Ezra Cornell.

On the second of July, 1862, Congress passed an act granting public lands to the several States and Territories which may provide Colleges for the benefit of Agriculture and the Mechanic Arts.

Under this act thirty thousand acres for each of its Senators and Representatives in Congress were appropriated to each State, and under this provision the share of the State of New York was in land scrip, representing 990,000 acres.

From the first, the State of New York determined to cease the policy of scattering its educational resources, and to concentrate this fund in a single institution worthy so great a Commonwealth.

Common sense, with the very signal failure of the State of Michigan in scattering such a fund, and her great success after concentrating it, were conclusive in favor of such a policy.

Acting upon this idea, the State first appropriated the entire amount of land scrip to the People's College upon certain very easy conditions. These conditions not being complied with, the Legislature by chapter 585, of the Laws of 1865, following the same policy of concentration, against much opposition and many attempts to scatter the fund, reaffirmed its old decision to concentrate the fund, by overwhelming majorities in each house, and gave the proceeds of the entire amount of scrip to the Cornell University on certain conditions, of which the most important were, that EZRA CORNELL should give to the Institution five hundred thousand dollars, and that one student should annually be received and educated, free of all charge for tuition, from each of the one hundred and twenty-eight Assembly Districts of the State, as a reward of merit for superior scholarship in the public schools or academies. Such student to be designated by a competitive examination, to be conducted on a plan laid down in the act.

At the first meeting of the trustees thereafter, Mr. CORNELL complied with the conditions of the charter by a gift of five hundred thousand dollars in due form. He then made the additional gift of two hundred acres of excellent land, with buildings, as a farm to be attached to the Agricultural Department; the Jewett collection in Geology and Palæontology, which had cost him ten thousand dollars, and since that time other gifts to the amount of twenty-five thousand dollars.

Besides this, Mr. CORNELL has expended about three hundred thousand dollars in purchasing the land scrip and locating the lands for the University, and it is proper to state here, that, previous to all these gifts, he had erected in the village of Ithaca, at a cost of nearly one hundred thousand dollars, a free public library with large halls, and with lecture rooms which will be exceedingly useful as affording supplementary accommodations for the lectures and public exercises of the University. Thus laying the foundation for a sure and large endowment, sufficient to enable the trustees to tender, as soon as the fund shall suffice, free board as well as instruction to the State Students.

RELATIONS OF THE UNIVERSITY TO THE STATE.

The act organizing the Cornell University makes it an organic part of the educational system of the State. The Governor, Lieutenant-Governor, Secretary of State, Superintendent of Public Instruction and Speaker of the House of Assembly are *ex officio* trustees. The President of the State Agricultural Society is also *ex officio* a member of the board.

It may be mentioned here, that the Board of Trustees are not a body sitting for life, but that they are constantly renewed, the term of office being five years; three being selected every year—one of them by the Alumni whenever they shall number fifty. This, it is hoped, will do much to ensure vigor and prevent the stagnation from which so many institutions of learning have suffered.

SCOPE OF THE UNIVERSITY.

The special departments referred to above will be developed conscientiously and as thoroughly as possible. The prominence plainly given the first two by the Act of Congress will be loyally remembered. It must also be constantly recollected that education is here to be made, not only scientific, but practical. Military education will also be provided for. Moreover, the trustees are also pledged to try fully and fairly the experiment of allowing students in appropriate departments to do something towards paying their way by organized manual labor, under scientific direction. This, however, will be voluntary, as the freedom of our University demands.

But beside these *special* departments, the trustees provide, in accordance with the clearly expressed intent of the Congressional act, *general* instruction., Mr. CORNELL's gift is made in order to round the whole institution into the proportions of an University worthy of the State. He expressed plainly and tersely the whole University theory when he said, "*I would found an institution where any person can find instruction in any study.*"

FEATURES OF THE UNIVERSITY.

First. Every effort will be made that the education given be practically useful. The idea of doing a student's mind some vague general good by studies which do not interest him, will not control. The constant policy will be to give mental discipline to every student *by studies which take practical hold* upon the tastes, aspirations and work of his life.

Second. There is to be University liberty of choice. Several courses carefully arranged will be presented, and the student, aided by friends and instructors, can make his choice among them.

When we consider that young men are constantly obliged to make choice unaided in regard to matters of even more difficulty and danger than courses of study, it will not be thought so absolutely necessary that but one single course should be allowed, and all men of all minds forced to fit it.

Third. There will be no Fetichism in regard to any single studies. All good studies will be allowed their due worth. While the beauty and worth of ancient classics will not be denied, it is hoped to give the study of modern classics, especially those of our own language, a far more important place than they have hitherto held in our colleges. Special attention will be paid to these.

Fourth. Historical studies and studies in Political and Social science will be held in high honor, and will have more attention than is usual in our higher institutions of learning. Beside thorough regular courses, it is intended to present special courses of lectures by non-resident professors of eminence.

Fifth. There will be no petty daily marking system, a pedantic device, which has eaten out from so many colleges all capacity among students to seek knowledge for knowledge's sake. Those professors will be sought who can stir enthusiasm, and who can thus cause students to do far more than under a perfunctory piecemeal study.

Sixth. It enters into the plan adopted by the Board of the Cornell University to bring about a closer and more manly intercourse and sympathy between Faculty and students than is usual in most of the colleges.

Seventh. The study of Human Anatomy, Physiology and Hygiene, with exercises for physical training, will be most carefully provided for.

Eighth. The Cornell University, as its highest aim, seeks to promote Christian civilization. *But it cannot be sectarian.* Established by a general government which recognizes no distinctions in creed, and by a citizen who holds the same view, it would be false to its trust were it to seek to promote any creed or to exclude any.

The State of New York, in designating this institution as the recipient of the bounty of the general government, has also declared the same doctrine. By the terms of the charter, no trustee, professor or student can be accepted or rejected on account of any religious or political opinions which he may or may not hold.

The success of the University of Michigan, where the Faculty comprises men of all religious sects and of all parties, is a sufficient refutation of those who assert that an institution of learning must be sectarian to be successful.

Access to the University Town.

The Cornell University is established at Ithaca, Tompkins county, New York. From the south, east and west, the most easy access is by the N. Y. and Erie Railway, leaving that road at Owego and taking the cars for Ithaca.

From the north, east and west, access is easy by the N. Y. Central Railroad, taking the "old road" between Rochester and Syracuse, and leaving it at Cayuga Bridge, whence steamboats run directly to Ithaca.

Any additional information can be obtained of Francis M. Finch, Secretary of the Board of Trustees, Ithaca, New York, or of Andrew D. White, President of the University, Syracuse, New York.

www.ingramcontent.com/pod-product-compliance
Lightning Source LLC
LaVergne TN
LVHW020635110826
845149LV00004B/1200

* 9 7 8 1 4 1 8 1 9 1 5 5 9 *